CAR LEASING SECRETS REVEALED

Today, leasing is the fastest growing form of financing private and business vehicles. Yet, most consumers have little or no knowledge about leasing, particularly how to negotiate more favorable rates and terms. However, that is all changed with the publication of *Lease Your Car For Less*, a consumers' guide to vehicle leasing. It's the book that car dealers and leasing companies didn't want published.

Lease Your Car For Less offers information heretofore guarded by the vehicle leasing industry. Consumers can now better understand exactly what a lease is, how lease costs are calculated, and what items in a lease can be negotiated to reduce its cost or improve its terms. Corporations that lease fleets of vehicles almost always negotiate with their leasing company. Now, consumers have the same opportunity.

Lease Your Car For Less introduces the vehicle leasing concept - what a lease is, and isn't. The differences between a lease and conventional bank auto loan are described. A complete chapter is devoted to describing how the lease process works. It also defines all the important leasing terms a consumer needs to understand in order to negotiate, successfully. Yet another chapter gives the reader an inside look at how leasing companies calculate the rates they charge. Sample calculations are provided for the reader to work through.

Finally, in a step-by-step walk through the actual leasing process, key negotiating points are highlighted, as are potential pitfalls to be avoided. The objective is to help the reader secure a lower lease cost and/or more advantageous terms. It's a fact. A well-negotiated lease can easily cost $50.00 to $150.00 *less* per month than a lease that hasn't been challenged.

Lease Your Car For Less is essential reading for anyone considering leasing as an alternative to bank or dealer financing. Its potential to save consumers hundreds, even thousands of dollars makes this information-packed publication worth the modest purchase price.

LEASE YOUR CAR FOR LESS

The Consumer's Guide To Vehicle Leasing

By Richard L. Kaye

2ND Edition

Library of Congress Catalog Card Number: 89-051069

ISBN 0-9623644-3-6

This edition published and printed in the United States of
America.

First Printing: August, 1989
2nd Edition: October, 1991

**A Special Thanks
To Automobile Manufacturers
In The U.S., Asia and Europe
Whose Egregiously High Prices
Have Assured The
Popularity Of Leasing**

Table of Contents

INTRODUCTION

W hen the first edition of <u>Lease Your Car For Less</u> hit the book stores in 1989, automobile leasing had already become popular among many U.S. buyers of luxury automobiles. During 1990, virtually all automobile manufacturers launched national advertising campaigns promoting leasing programs not only for their high-priced models, but for virtually all models in their line. Local dealers began running ad blitzes of their own, as did independent leasing companies and even a few banks. Clearly, leasing was on its way to becoming a mainstream form of financing an automobile purchase.

Why? The best answer is that the American public and automotive industry marketing gurus simultaneously arrived at the same conclusion: for many consumers, leasing has important advantages over buying. Leasing can mean lower monthly payments, no sizeable down payment, and no worry about trade-in value. For car dealers, leasing can move inventory when the economy is slumping.

The purpose of this book

Leasing offers certain economic benefits over conventional bank or dealer financing, or the outright purchase of an automobile. However, unless you understand how a lease is structured, how to evaluate its economics, what pitfalls to avoid, and how to negotiate the most advantageous lease agreement, you may leave yourself vulnerable to an incredibly bad deal.

The purpose of this book is to help you save money - large amounts of money. How? Simply, by helping you become a better-informed consumer on the subject of automobile leasing. The small amount of time you'll invest in this book should help you determine if leasing is right for you or your business, and if so, how to get the best deal on a lease.

A caveat: Along with leasing's growing popularity has come a corresponding growth in the number of leasing companies. All are vying for your business. The good news is, you'll benefit from healthy competition. The bad news is, you may be offered deals that are too good to be true. Take advantage of the former by being informed, and watch out for the latter the same way.

How to use this book

It is assumed that you are neither a Certified Public Accountant, nor holder of an MBA in finance. Therefore, the ideas and information presented in this book are intentionally simplified, but not oversimplified. In other words, relevant information will not be ignored or omitted for simplicity's sake. It will, however, be presented in lay terms so as to be understandable and usable the first time through.

It is also assumed that you probably don't like the "dealing" part of buying a new car, but that you understand the **Theory of Reality**[1]. This theory says that, in reality, things aren't the way you'd like them to be, nor the way they appear to be, but the way they are. The theory also states that you either acknowledge reality and use it to your benefit or it will automatically work against you.

When purchasing an automobile, whether or not you intend to lease, the reality of the transaction has the seller trying to get more, rather than less, of your money. It is the seller's goal to make it appear that you're getting the best deal. But, it is also the seller's goal to *sell* the vehicle. Your goal, therefore, is to challenge the seller to take as little of your money as possible and still deliver the car to you.

This book is divided into five chapters. Each chapter deals with one aspect of the automobile leasing process. It is strongly recommended that you read each chapter and review its contents before moving on to the next. You may find it helpful to keep a pocket calculator handy so you'll be able to work through the calculations used in several examples.

The knowledge of leasing you'll acquire through this book should give you an important advantage when it's time to begin negotiating your lease. Used properly, this advantage could save you hundreds, perhaps thousands of dollars.

[1] Ringer, Robert J., *Winning Through Intimidation*, Fawcett Crest, 1974, pp 31

GLOSSARY OF VEHICLE LEASING TERMS

Advance payment: One or more monthly payments paid at the beginning of the lease term, usually one month before the first regular monthly payment is due.

Annual percentage rate: Simple interest for one year.

APR equivalent method: A method used to calculate lease rate using a complex computer program.

Cap cost factor method: A method used to calculate lease rate using a money factor.

Capital reduction: Any money paid by the lessee to lower the vehicle purchase price. Usually the trade-in value of a used car.

Closed-end lease: The vehicle is returned to the lessor at lease end with no further lessee obligation.

Constant yield method: A method used to calculate lease rate using a conventional interest rate.

Depreciation: The difference between a vehicle's purchase price and residual value.

Disposition fee: A surcharge applied to the basic lease cost by a lessor to cover costs associated with return of the vehicle at lease end.

Early termination fee: A surcharge or penalty for terminating a lease before its normal expiration date.

Excess mileage fee: A surcharge to the basic lease payment, usually based on a per-mile rate, for any mileage driven in excess of a predetermined amount during the lease term.

Gap insurance: Additional coverage for the difference between a vehicle's regular insurance benefit and what is owed on a lease.

Lease fee: See Lease rate.

Lease initiation fee: A surcharge applied to the basic lease cost by a lessor to cover administrative costs, sales commissions, or to add revenue.

Lease rate: The equivalent of a bank's finance charge. Typically based upon the lessor's cost of money and desired profit on the lease.

Lease term: Number of months the vehicle is on lease.

Lessee: Party who pays a lessor for the use of the vehicle.

Lessor: Party who purchases and owns the vehicle that will be used by the lessee

Money factor: A decimal, usually four digits, which is used to calculate a lease rate. The interest equivalent is found by multiplying by 24.

M.S.R.P.: Manufacturers Suggested Retail Price

Open-end lease: The vehicle is purchased by the lessee at lease end, or the lessee requests that the vehicle be sold on his behalf.

Residual value: Selling price of vehicle at lease end.

Sales tax: State and local taxes on the vehicle purchase price.

Security deposit: Usually the equivalent of one month's lease payment, paid in advance and refundable at lease end.

Vehicle purchase price: Manufacturer's suggested retail price less discounts, rebates and cap reductions.

Vendor: Entity that provides the leased vehicle.

1

WHAT A VEHICLE LEASE IS. . .AND ISN'T.

A vehicle lease gives you the right to use a specific vehicle for a specific length of time in return for payment of a specific amount of money. You could think of a lease as a rental agreement; you would be reasonably correct. In a lease you pay for use of the vehicle to the extent that it depreciates in value, plus some additional amount regarded as profit for the lease holder.

Ordinarily, there are three parties to a vehicle lease: 1) the seller or vendor; 2) the lessor; and, 3) the lessee. To understand what a lease is, you need to know what role each party plays.

The Seller or Vendor

This is usually the automobile dealer whose role is to sell the car. In some instances, it can be the vehicle's manufacturer. In a lease transaction, the seller or vendor won't actually sell the car to you, although you will take delivery of the vehicle. The actual sale and transfer of title on the vehicle will be made to the lessor.

The Lessor

This is the vehicle's real owner. The lessor purchases the vehicle from the seller (dealer or manufacturer), receives title to the vehicle, and then turns the vehicle over to you for a specified period of use at a fixed monthly rental rate. When the lease reaches the end of its term, and depending upon the type of lease, the lessor will sell the vehicle to you or will take possession of the vehicle and attempt to sell it to someone else.

Lessors come in all shapes and sizes. Many banks have established leasing subsidiaries, as have finance companies. Most automobile manufacturers have their own leasing companies. And, there are thousands of independent leasing companies who are financed by insurance companies, banks, private investors, foreign capital sources, or their own capital.

The Lessee

You are the lessee. You will take delivery of the vehicle from the seller, but you will not own it. Instead, you will make monthly rental payments to the lessor for use of the vehicle. When the lease period ends, you will either purchase the vehicle from the lessor, or return the vehicle to the lessor or his agent with no further obligation.

Thus, a lease differs from a conventional bank or finance company auto loan in that a third party (the lessor) makes an outright purchase of the vehicle for the purpose of renting it to you. A bank or finance company, on the other hand, loans you the money to make your own purchase and holds title to the car as collateral on the loan.

Another major difference, albeit slightly more technical, deals with how much you pay. With a conventional bank or finance company loan, you agree to repay the entire purchase price of the vehicle, less your down payment, plus interest. With a lease, you pay for the purchase price of the vehicle, less what the lessor expects to receive for the vehicle when he sells it at the conclusion of your lease, plus a profit for the lessor. The vehicle's selling price at the end of your lease is also known as the '**Residual Value**.'

Table 1 illustrates the basic difference in cost between a lease and a conventional auto loan. It compares a 36 month bank loan requiring a 20% down payment with a 36 month lease that assumes a residual value of $10,000. For this illustration, we assume a zero percent interest rate (no profit for the investor) on both instruments and no extraordinary fees, taxes or service charges.

TABLE 1

	Conventional Loan	Lease
Selling price of vehicle	$ 25,000.	$ 25,000.
Your down-payment (20%)	$ 5,000.	-0-
Residual value of vehicle after 36 months	N/A[2]	$ 10,000.
Principal amount upon which your payments are based	$ 20,000.	$ 15,000.
Monthly principal repayment amount based on 36 months	$ 555.	$ 416.

[2] The value of your car at trade-in time is not a factor when computing the amount of your loan.

Note that the principal amount of the lease is lower than that of the loan. Therefore, the monthly repayment of principal will be lower. Herein lies one of the major advantages of leasing: lower monthly payments. Another advantage: no down payment is required, so you retain the use of the money for other purposes.

Lease types

There are two basic forms of a lease: **closed-end** and **open-end**. The differences are important for you to understand.

The **closed-end lease** requires that you: 1) return the vehicle at the end of the lease term with no further financial obligation, or 2) purchase it at a predetermined price which was established when the lease agreement was first made. This is known as an option to buy.

The **open-end lease** also allows you to turn-in the vehicle or purchase it when the lease expires. Should you desire to purchase the car, you'll pay the retail fair market value. Should you elect to turn the car back to the lessor, you'll be obligated to pay any difference between its residual value and the actual fair market value at lease termination. This assumes that the car's market value is less than its residual. The risk of a sizeable payment at termination is why consumers should avoid an open-end lease.

The advantages and disadvantages of each type of lease will be discussed in greater detail in a later chapter.

In summary. . .

• A lease is based upon a third party purchase of your vehicle and your payment to the owner for its use over a fixed time.

• A loan is based upon your purchase of the vehicle using someone else's money and agreeing to repay the money over a fixed time.

• A car lease is a contract to pay for the use of the vehicle.

• A car loan is a contract to repay someone for the use of their money.

• A lease is not a loan.

2

HOW A LEASE WORKS.

Mr. Green is ready for a new car. He has chosen the make and model he'd like to drive, and has decided that he wants to lease it rather than buy it. (Author's note: In chapter 5, you will find helpful information on making the lease versus purchase decision. For now, please assume that Mr. Green's decision was a prudent one.)

Now, it's time for Mr. Green to visit a few dealers and do some serious shopping. At this stage, there is absolutely no difference between leasing or buying. Mr. Green's only objective is to get the *lowest purchase price* possible from one or more worthy dealers. By obtaining the same or a similar price from several dealers, Mr. Green affords himself more bargaining power to get the best lease deal.

Once Mr. Green is satisfied that he has negotiated for the lowest purchase price from a dealer, he then advises the dealer that he wishes to lease the vehicle. The dealer will ask Mr. Green several questions:

"How long do you want the lease to run?"

"Will you or your business lease the car?"

"When the lease ends, do you want to purchase the car?"

Mr. Green elects to lease for three years (not coincidentally, the car he wants has a three year warranty). He will lease it through his business and has no plan to buy the car at the end of the lease term.

With this information, the dealer proceeds to compute the monthly cost of Mr. Green's lease. Since most dealers offer leases through third party lessors, it is common for the dealer to check several sources for the best rates and terms. When computations are completed, the dealer reports back to Mr. Green:

> *"Mr. Green, your 36 month lease will cost you $459.00 per month. Your total outlay will be $16,524.00. You are allowed 15,000 miles per year or 45,000 total miles. There is an excess mileage charge of $.08 per mile in excess of 45,000. A lease origination fee of $300.00 and security deposit equal to one month's rental are required. The security deposit will be refunded at the end of the lease. We'll need your first month's rental payment when the lease is signed. And, we'll also need some credit information on you and your business."*

In response to this "offer," Mr. Green makes written notes on the terms and conditions of the lease. He advises the dealer that he'll consider the offer. Then, Mr. Green goes to the second dealer with whom he has been working. He advises that the purchase price is acceptable and that he wishes to lease. The scenario repeats itself and now Mr. Green has two lease offers to compare and consider. He also has a perfect opportunity to place both dealers into a competitive bidding situation by using one offer to gain concessions on the other and vice versa.

After a few phone calls, dealer visits, and some aggressive negotiating, Mr. Green decides that one of the two lease offers is acceptable. He advises the dealer, who proceeds to fill out a vehicle lease application. Mr. Green signs the application and writes a check for the first month's rental and refundable security deposit. The lease origination fee will be included in the monthly lease payment. The next day Mr. Green provides copies of his latest business financial statement and proof of personal income to the dealer. He then awaits approval of the lease application from the lessor.

Within 24 hours, approval from the lessor is received by the dealer. Essentially, the lessor has agreed to purchase the vehicle from the dealer at the stipulated price and rent it to Mr. Green for 36 months at $459.00 per month. The dealer calls Mr. Green to advise that the lease has been approved and that the car will be ready for pick-up by 5:00 PM. Mr. Green's signature will be required on the lease contract and a few additional documents.

Each and every month for the next 36 months, Mr. Green's business sends a $459.00 payment to the lessor. About 32 months into the lease, Mr. Green receives a letter from the lessor advising that the lease will end in four months. The lessor asks Mr. Green to advise whether he wishes to extend the lease and keep the car for an additional time period, or turn it in. (Author's note: most closed-end leases can be extended from several months to more than a year. Monthly payments may remain the same, or may change due to economic factors affecting the lessor.) Mr. Green advises that he'll turn it in before the end of the 36th month, which he does.

At turn-in time, the dealer inspects the car for damage and unusual wear. There is none. Its mileage is 42,505 so there won't be an excess mileage charge. Mr. Green cleans out the glove compartment and trunk, turns in his keys, receives a check for his refundable security deposit, and leaves the dealership. For Mr. Green, the transaction is over, while the lessor must now find a buyer for the car. Typically, the lessor will first offer the car to the dealer who received it.

The lessor must recover at least the residual amount he predicted on Mr. Green's lease. Any amount greater than the residual increases the lessor's total earnings on the transaction. It is a fact: most lessors depend upon receiving the predicted, or greater-than-predicted, residual in order to make leasing worthwhile as an investment.

3

HOW THE LEASE RENTAL RATE IS CALCULATED

In order to negotiate your best deal on a leased vehicle, it is necessary to understand how a car dealer (usually acting on behalf of the lessor), or an independent leasing company, calculates the monthly rental rate you'll be charged.

There are five variables which determine the rental rate for any lease:

1. Vehicle purchase price
2. Vehicle residual value
3. Lease rate or lease fee
4. Extraordinary fees, taxes and service charges
5. Lease term

1. Vehicle purchase price is exactly that - the negotiated price at which the dealer is willing to sell you the vehicle. Some dealers may tell you that a lease is always based on the manufacturer's suggested retail price (MSRP) of the vehicle. *Don't believe it.* You should work just as hard on negotiating the *lowest* purchase price for a leased vehicle as a purchased vehicle. True, you are negotiating on behalf of the lessor. However, the payments you make to the lessor will, in part, be determined by the final purchase price. Consider that a $1,000 difference in the purchase price could cost you - or save you - about $27.77 per month over a three year lease. So, be certain you are getting all the discounts and incentive rebates being offered.

Vehicle purchase price also takes into consideration whether or not you trade-in a used car. You may elect to take the cash value for the trade-in, or you may choose to apply the money against the new car purchase price to further lower it. This is called a **capital reduction** or cap reduction for short.

Finally, purchase price can also include extraordinary fees, taxes and service charges. These costs can be paid out-of-pocket, or more likely, will be added to the purchase price before your lease cost is calculated. More information on extraordinary fees taxes and service charges can be found later in this chapter.

2. Vehicle residual value is the price that the lessor *expects* to receive when he sells the vehicle at the end of its lease period. The lessor may try to sell the vehicle to the dealer from whom it was originally purchased, or may attempt to sell it through other channels.

Residual value is always based on a percentage of the automobile's M.S.R.P. (sticker price) <u>less</u> any soft costs such as freight or preparation charges. While manufacturers generally set and publish residual percentage factors at the beginning of a model year, they are subject to change as market conditions change. For example, if a car sells better than predicted and demand exceeds supply, the residual factor may be increased.

Most lessors use a standard automotive industry reference such as the *Automotive Leasing Guide*, the *Kelley Blue Book*, the *Black Book Leasing Guide*, or the *National Automobile Dealers Association Official Used Car Guide* as a guide to projected resale prices. Generally, the prices in these guides do not vary by a significant amount from one guide to the next.

In a lease, a *higher* residual value means a lower monthly rental payment for you. Your monthly payment will, in part, be based upon the vehicle's depreciation: the difference between the new vehicle's purchase price and its residual value. For example: a $20,000 purchase price less an $8,000 residual value means your monthly payments will be based on $12,000 of depreciation. If the residual value is increased to $8,500, your payments will be based on $11,500 of depreciation. On a three year lease, the $500 difference equates to a $13.88 reduction in your monthly payment.

3. Lease rate or lease fee is the finance charge you will pay the lessor. It is the same as an interest rate which is applied to the combined <u>total</u> of the vehicle's purchase price plus residual value.

A lessor, or car dealer representing the lessor, will probably not voluntarily disclose the lease rate or lease fee to you. They are not obligated by law to do so. Instead, they will usually quote you a monthly lease payment which includes the interest charge.

This raises an interesting and very appropriate question: Exactly how much "interest" are you being charged? You'd certainly want to know if you went to a bank for a conventional auto loan, so why not a lease?

Although the law favors the lessor, do not hesitate to ask. In fact, demand to know. Any reluctance to disclose the lease rate should be considered an attempt to hide something. Walk away from the deal.

Your lease rate will be quoted as a monthly or total dollar amount, an interest rate or a **"money factor."** You may wish to convert from one form to another in order to compare different deals. Here's how. The numbers used are only to help illustrate the calculations:

•To convert dollars to a money factor and then to an annual percentage rate (A.P.R.):

1) If you are quoted a total dollar amount (example: $4,499.64), divide by the months in your lease (example: 36) to get the monthly amount ($124.99).

2) Divide the monthly amount by the combined total of the purchase price (example: $20,000) plus residual value (example: $8,000). Your answer ($124.99 divided by $28,000.00) will be a decimal of at least four places (.00446). This is the **money factor.**

3) Multiply the money factor by 24 (.107) and move the decimal point in your answer two places right [10.7]. This is the **annual percentage rate.**

•**If you are quoted a "money factor" and wish to express
  it as an annual percentage rate:**
  1) Multiply the money factor by 24. For example: money
  factor = .00446 x 24 = .1070 = 10.7%.

• **If you are quoted an annual percentage rate and wish
  to know the money factor:**
  1) Convert the interest rate to a decimal and divide by 24.
  Example: 10.7% = .107 / 24 = .00446.

Caution: if the interest rate used to calculate your lease fee
is substantially higher than current rates being charged by
banks on conventional home equity or auto loans, you may
be paying too much even though your monthly payments
are lower.

4. Extraordinary fees, taxes and service charges are to be
expected with almost any lease from a dealer or independent
leasing company. They include:

• *Lease initiation fee:* a service charge, usually added-on by
  the leasing company as added revenue or to cover
  commissions paid to the dealer.
• *Sales taxes:* although they vary from state to state, taxes are
  as much as part of a lease as they are an outright purchase.
  In a lease, you may elect to include taxes in your monthly
  payment, or pay them up-front, in cash.
• *Disposition fee:* another service charge. This one occurs at
  the end of the lease when it is time to turn-in your vehicle.
  It is not normally included in your lease payment.
• *Vehicle title and registration fee:* varies from state to state,
  and cannot be avoided. This fee is often included in the lease
  payment.
• *Other taxes:* including excise, rental/use, and personal
  property taxes. These vary from city to county to state.

In almost every lease transaction, the aforementioned extra-ordinary fees, taxes and service charges are added to your total cost of depreciation before monthly payments are calculated. As such, these costs will affect the total cost of your lease, and can affect your monthly payment amount if you choose to have them included. Some of these costs are negotiable as you will learn in the next chapter.

5. Lease term is the length of the lease. Most car leases run from two to five years. The longer your lease term, the lower your monthly payments. However, a longer lease means you'll pay more interest. It also means you may be stuck with a car that requires extensive repairs long beyond the expiration of the warranty period. Lease term is a variable that needs to be given careful consideration.

How the variables are used to calculate what your lease payments will be.

While there are several different methods which lessors and dealers use to compute the payments on a lease, you can use the following formula to determine what you should be paying on a conventional (no gimmicks) lease. There are four simple calculations which you need to make:

1) calculate the monthly depreciation and taxes you'll pay;
2) calculate the monthly amount of interest being charged;
3) calculate the monthly total of depreciation and interest;
4) calculate the total of all payments over the life of the lease.

It is important to note that sales tax, luxury tax, gas guzzler tax, registration fees, and other licensing costs will normally be included in the purchase price of the car. When you calculate depreciation, you'll actually be including these costs. Table 2 describes each of the four calculations.

TABLE 2

Assume the following details:
- Purchase price: 19,000.00 incl. taxes
- Residual value: 8,000.00
- Lease term: 36 months
- Money factor: .00446 (10.7% A.P.R.)

1) Calculate monthly depreciation

Purchase Price:	$19,000.00
Less - Residual:	- 8,000.00
Equals - Depreciation:	11,000.00
Divided by - Term:	36
Equals - Deprec/Mo.:	$ 305.55

2) Calculate monthly interest charge

Purchase price:	$19,000.00
Plus - Residual:	8,000.00
Equals - Total Money:	27,000.00
Times - Money Factor:	.00446
Equals - Interest/Mo.:	$ 120.42

3) Calculate monthly total

Depreciation/Mo.:	$ 305.55
Plus - Interest/Mo.:	120.42
Equals - Monthly pmt:	$ 425.97

4) Calculate total payments

Monthly payment:	$425.97
Times - Term:	36
Equals - Total Cost:	$15,334.92

Note on sales taxes

If you are comparing deals from dealers or leasing companies in different towns or counties, where local tax rates may differ, you may wish to have each lessor or dealer compute your lease payment without including taxes. This will enable you to make an apples-to-apples comparison of costs between companies. After the fact, you should decide whether or not to include taxes in your lease payment. Most lessors will automatically assume that you wish to have sales taxes included rather than paid out-of-pocket. Given the changes in tax laws regarding the deductability of sales tax, they may be right. After 1991, there will be no personal deduction.

In making your decision, remember that sales taxes and vehicle registration costs, which are included in your lease, will be lumped in with depreciation when the monthly lease rate is calculated, so you'll actually be paying interest on the sales tax. However, you won't be losing the use of your money for the life of the lease, so the cost may be justified.

4

NEGOTIATING YOUR BEST LEASE DEAL

As covered in Chapter 3, there are five variables which are used to determine your monthly lease cost: 1) purchase price; 2) residual value; 3) lease rate; 4) extraordinary fees, taxes and service charges;and, 5) lease term. In order to negotiate your best lease deal, you'll need to know how each variable affects your lease cost, and which ones are subject to negotiation.

Unfortunately, the answer doesn't come easily. While you may find that a reduction in the lease rate has the greatest gross effect on lowering your payments, the lessor may not be willing to negotiate his rate, in which case you'll have to work with the other four variables to create a reduction to your payment. The tables, below, demonstrate the effects of each variable on a particular lease transaction.

How Each Variable Affects A Lease

Vehicle Purchase Price: Check the chart below to determine the amount your monthly payment decreases for every $100 *reduction* in purchase price.

<table>
<tr><td colspan="5" align="center">Lease Term</td></tr>
<tr><td>1 Year</td><td>2 Year</td><td>3 Year</td><td>4 Year</td><td>5 Year</td></tr>
<tr><td>$ 8.33</td><td>$ 4.16</td><td>$ 2.77</td><td>$ 2.08</td><td>$ 1.67</td></tr>
</table>

Vehicle Residual Value: Check the chart below to determine the amount your monthly payment decreases for every $100 *increase* in residual value.

Lease Term

1 Year	2 Year	3 Year	4 Year	5 Year
$ 8.33	$ 4.16	$ 2.77	$ 2.08	$ 1.67

Lease Rate or Lease Fee

As stated in the last chapter, the lessor makes most of his money on the interest you are being charged. Thus, a change in the lease rate can have the greatest positive or negative impact on the cost of your lease. For example, on a car costing $20,000 with an $8,000 residual value, a reduction from 10.7% to 10.2% on a 36 month lease saves $209.52.

At the risk of being repetitive, remember: unless you know how much interest is being charged, you risk paying more than you should. So, if the lessor or dealer isn't willing to tell you the actual rate, or at least give you enough information to make your own calculation, find another deal.

Extraordinary Fees, Taxes and Service Charges: Total all costs and divide by the number of months on your lease term. This will give you an approximate cost per month. However, it is important to remember that these extraordinary costs are subject to an interest charge when they are included in the vehicle purchase price and depreciation cost is calculated. Regardless, you can use the approximate cost per month for comparison purposes.

Lease term: While your lease term isn't negotiated, you must be careful to select the term which will best suit your needs. A shorter term means higher monthly payments, but less total interest and a shorter commitment to the vehicle. A longer lease term means lower monthly payments, but more total interest and a longer commitment to the vehicle. Unless you are forced to seek the lowest possible monthly payment, a 36 to 48 month lease is probably best. Payments will be relatively low and most warranties now cover this period. Table 3 illustrates how lease term affects your payments.

TABLE 3

How monthly payments are affected by the lease term

Assume a vehicle purchase price of $20,000 with 0% interest and a theoretical depreciation schedule.

	Residual Value	Accumulated Depreciation	Monthly Payment
Year 1:	$ 17,000	$ 3,000	$ 250.00
Year 2:	14,500	5,500	229.16
Year 3:	12,500	7,500	208.33
Year 4:	11,000	9,000	187.50
Year 5:	10,000	10,000	166.66

It's Time To Negotiate!

To negotiate the best deal possible on a lease, the following steps must be followed:

1. Negotiate the lowest purchase price on the vehicle.
2. Dispose of your trade-in vehicle if one exists.
3. Advise the dealer you wish to lease.
4. Set forth the terms of the lease.
5. Negotiate the elements of the lease.
6. Review and execute the lease agreement.

Commentary on Steps 1 through 3

1. Negotiate the lowest purchase price on the vehicle,

2. Dispose of your trade-in vehicle if one exists.

3. Advise the dealer you wish to lease.

This discussion assumes that you have selected the vehicle of your choice. Now it is time to negotiate with your dealer for the best possible purchase price. It is prudent to check prices with several dealers before deciding from whom you will purchase. There are several very good books on the subject of negotiating the best purchase price with a dealer. ***REMEMBER: do not disclose your intentions to lease while you are negotiating the purchase price.***

Once you have negotiated the lowest possible purchase price, you may have to decide whether to trade-in or sell your present vehicle. Here, too, your goal is to obtain the best price possible. However, regardless of whether you trade-in or sell, the proceeds can be used to reduce the cost of your lease by reducing the amount to be financed. As you'll recall, this is called a **capital reduction.**

If you elect to trade-in, it is suggested that you advise the dealer *after* you have negotiated your best purchase price, but *before* you advise the dealer of your desire to lease. This will help assure you that the dealer will not hold your trade-in as "hostage" against the agreed-to purchase price. That is, the dealer will not be as inclined to offer less on your trade.

It is now time to advise the dealer that you wish to lease the vehicle. No formal notification is required; just tell your sales person of your intentions. They may or may not try to talk you out of leasing. If they do, usually they will cite economic reasons, stating that leasing is more costly than purchasing. They may be right. But, as was mentioned in an earlier chapter, leasing offers other economic benefits which may outweigh the pure cost of the transaction.

Commentary on Step 4

4. Set forth the terms of the lease.

You have advised the dealer of your desire to lease. Now it is time to determine what the lease will cost you. In order to compute a lease cost, the dealer will need to know the terms of the lease you desire. Specifically, you will have to advise the dealer on the following:

1) whether you want a closed-end or open-end lease;
2) the lease's firm-term (how many years the lease will run); and,
3) whether you will make any capital reduction to the purchase price.

Closed-end versus open-end leases

The most common lease, which is probably best for most consumers and small business operators, is the closed-end lease. It's also known as a net or fixed-cost lease. In it, you agree to pay a set, monthly amount and when the lease ends, you either turn-in the car and walk away or buy the car at a price which was pre-set at the time you entered into the lease (buy-out option).

A word about the buy-out option on a closed-end lease: **be sure the buy-out price is written into your contract and it's the same as the residual value which should also be written into your contract.** If the buy-out price is higher than the residual value it usually means the residual is set too low and you're paying for too much depreciation.

An *open-end* lease, sometimes called a *finance* or *equity* lease, stipulates that you can purchase the vehicle at the end of the lease for, 1) a stated amount, or 2) the fair market retail value. If you choose an open-end lease and decide not to purchase the vehicle, you can ask the dealer to sell it for you. Should the car sell for more than the purchase price stated in the lease, you would pay off the amount due on the lease and keep any excess.

However, if it sells for less, you must make up the difference out-of-pocket. In 1976, the federal government passed the Consumer Leasing Act. This legislation limits the out-of-pocket payment to no more than three times the monthly lease payment assuming that there is no excess use, wear or damage to the vehicle. But, beware, the lessor can sue to collect more if he feels so justified. This is a major drawback to an open-end lease and why you should (probably) avoid one.

A final word on open-end leases: because you assume part of the financial risk should the vehicle be worth less at lease termination, monthly payments are usually lower than on a closed-end lease.

Selecting the lease's term

Generally, vehicle leases run from one to five years. Longer terms are sometimes offered, usually by independent lessors. The longer the term, the lower the monthly payments, even though more depreciation must be financed.

Your monthly payment is only one criterion for selecting a particular lease term. Others include: 1) interest rate trends, 2) vehicle warranty, and 3) the length of time you are willing to drive the same car.

A note on warranties: since you will be responsible for the cost of all routine (not covered by insurance) maintenance and repairs, it is always a prudent idea to lease for the length of the warranty or less. For example, select up to a three year lease if the vehicle carries a three year warranty. This will minimize your out-of-pocket expenses on out-of-warranty repairs.

If you elect to lease for longer than the warranty period, you may wish to consider an extended warranty policy and try to get the dealer or lessor to pay its cost or discount the premium as part of your deal.

Making a Capital Reduction

A ''Cap Reduction'' reduces the gross cost of your vehicle's purchase price. Proceeds from a trade-in or out-of-pocket cash can be used. Either way, the net effect of a "Cap Reduction" is to lower your monthly payments and reduce the amount of interest you'll be paying to the lessor.

For example, suppose you negotiate a price of $20,000 for a new car. You sell or trade-in your old car and receive $5,000. This "capital" can be applied against the $20,000 to reduce the financed amount to $15,000 and, thus, reduce your monthly lease rental payments.

Remember, however, that you are also losing the use of this money for other investment purposes. This is a cost (referred to as an opportunity cost) which must be factored into the total cost of your lease.

At this point, your dealer or the leasing company has all the information needed to calculate your lease payments and the total lease cost. The calculation will be made approximately as described in Chapter 3.

Commentary on Step 5

5. Negotiate the elements of the lease.

Notice that Step 5 says to negotiate the elements of the lease rather than the monthly cost of the lease. Remember, there are five variables which lessors use to calculate your lease cost: 1) purchase price, 2) residual value, 3) lease rate, and 4) extraordinary fees, taxes and service charges; and, 5)lease term. FOUR OF THE FIVE VARIABLES - PURCHASE PRICE, RESIDUAL VALUE, EXTRAORDINARY FEES, AND LEASE TERM - ARE ALMOST ALWAYS SUBJECT TO NEGOTIATION.

At this point in the transaction, it is assumed that you have already negotiated for the best vehicle purchase price. Therefore, you are left with only three variables - residual value, extraordinary fees and lease term - on which you may be able to exert influence.

Negotiating a higher residual value

In the event you feel your monthly payments are too high, negotiate with the lessor for a higher residual value to lower the amount of depreciation being financed. Check with various leasing sources to determine who is quoting the highest residual value on the car of your choice. Use this information to substantiate your claim that the residual should be higher. You may even want to check with dealers and lessors in states other than yours. Often the same car is worth more at trade-in time in certain geographic regions.

You'll recall that there are four or more reference guides used by dealers and lessors to determine wholesale and retail used car values. Ask which guide your lessor used. Ask him to check other guides, or consult with other lessors to determine which guide(s) they use. Either way, make sure your lessor is quoting the highest residual value.

Negotiating reductions in extraordinary fees and service charges.

Taxes, title and registration fee are not normally subject to reduction. However, you may be able to secure reductions or waivers on a variety of special charges. Many, if not most, are fair game for negotiating. However, in order to know which of these are negotiable, you must first know which are applicable to your particular lease. Ask the right questions to find out:

* Is there a lease initiation (acquisition) fee?
* Is there an end-of-lease disposition fee?
* Is there a security deposit required?
* Is there an advance payment required? If so, how much?
* Who pays for title and registration fees?
* How much mileage per year is allowed? What is the rate per mile for any excess mileage at the end of the lease?
* Who is responsible for maintenance and repairs?
* What are the penalties, if any, for ending the lease early?

Once you have secured the answers to these questions, you can decide which points to negotiate. A discussion of each issue follows:

1. Lease initiation fee: Most lessors ask for a fee associated with creating the lease. Some call it an admisistrative fee while others combine it with "Gap" insurance. This fee can be a pure profit-maker. Check it carefully.

2. Lease disposition fee - Many lessors require payment of a special end-of-lease fee at the time you turn-in your car. A $250 fee is not unusual. This should be the first special charge you negotiate to have waived. It is a pure adder to lessor or dealer profit.

3. Security deposit - Most lessors require a security deposit equivalent to one or two months' payments. Your options are to have this payment waived or have interest paid on the deposit while it is being held by the lessor. Security deposits are an important source of revenue to the lessor if you allow them to hold your money, interest-free. Consider that a $500.00 security deposit, invested at 8% compounded for four years, earns about $235.00 in interest for the lessor. Or, looking at it from a different perspective, your $500.00 security deposit can be used by the lessor as his own form of "Cap Reduction" to lower the amount he must pay out-of-pocket to the dealer. Thus, his costs are reduced and profit increases. It is often easy to negotiate bank rate interest on your security deposit. Don't be bashful!

4. Advance payment - Many lessors require an advance payment equal to one months' lease payment. Normally, this payment would not be due until the end of the first month. However, the lessor earns interest on your money for the extra 30 days, thereby increasing his total revenue. By all means, negotiate a waiver of any advance payments.

5. Title and registration fees - Depending upon where you live, fees can be $100.00 or more. The vehicle's title and registration will be in the lessor's name. However, fees are usually passed on to the lessee. If you are able to avoid these charges, you're that much ahead.

A special note to those of you with "Vanity" (special number) license plates: When you lease, a new set of plates will be issued in your lessor's name by your state's department of motor vehicles. If you wish to have special plates on your leased car, you will have to apply for a change of plates *after* you receive the original registration and license plates. That's an added cost to you unless you can get the lessor to pick up the cost. No harm in trying!

6. Mileage - Most lease contracts stipulate a *maximum* number of miles per year on the vehicle. A common figure is 15,000 miles. Thus, on a three year lease, the maximum number of miles allowed would be 45,000. Any excess mileage is usually charged on a per-mile basis. Thus, if you drive more miles per year than allowed, you'll do well to negotiate 1) a waiver of the mileage restriction, 2) an increase in the mileage allotment, 3) a reduction in the cost per excess mile to be charged, or 4) some suitable combination of the above variables.

7. Maintenance and repairs - Most lease agreements stipulate that the lessee is responsible for all maintenance and repairs. It is uncommon for a lessor to share in these costs. However, some lessors may be willing to absorb some portion of the costs in exchange for an additional charge. If you are able to negotiate with the lessor for relief from these charges, you'll be way ahead of the game. However, the best strategy remains to lease for the life of the warranty or less.

8. Penalty for early termination - All lease agreements include a potentially dangerous section called: Voluntary Early Termination or simply Early Termination. This section includes the terms and conditions under which you may end your lease prior to the stated lease termination date.

It is not unusual that you might wish to end your lease early.

For example, suppose the manufacturer of the vehicle you're driving introduces a flashy new body style. You may want to trade-in before your current lease is over. Or, there may be some unfortunate economic reason why you need to put the brakes on your monthly payments. Whatever the situation, most leases have a provision for early termination. But, beware, the cost can be astronomical.

Some early termination clauses are licenses to the sun, the moon and the stars. Consider the following clause taken from a Mercedes-Benz Credit Corporation lease agreement:

> *"I understand that I may not terminate this lease prior to expiration of the lease term unless Mercedes-Benz Credit Corporation has first agreed to such termination and I agree to be bound to any terms Mercedes-Benz Credit Corporation may impose in connection with such termination..."*

Many lease agreements cite one or more methods by which your cost of early termination is determined. Most use a system which computes costs using two formulae. The lessee pays the greater of the two costs. The first formula uses the vehicle's "fair market (average trade-in) value - less the vehicle's original purchase price - plus any repair or reconditioning costs. The second formula calculates the sum of the remaining lease payments - less lease charges ("interest") and sales taxes - plus any lease disposition charges - less the projected wholesale value of the car at the normal end of the lease term - plus any government fees and taxes associated with early termination - plus any costs to repair or recondition the vehicle.

It isn't hard to see why early termination can be a complicated and costly proposition, and why you should try to negotiate more favorable terms before signing the contract (even if you do not anticipate an early termination situation). For example, where the lessor wishes to charge the *greater* of the two computed values in the above example, negotiate for the *lower* of the two computations and you may save a bundle. An even better idea is to negotiate with your dealer or lessor to guarantee - in writing - that you can terminate early without penalties or responsibility for any of the residual. Push hard for a deal in which your pay-off amount would be equal to that of a conventional bank loan at the lease's effective interest rate, for the same car, at the same capitalized cost (purchase price on which the lease was based), with the same number of months remaining.

If you are successful in negotiating for this valuable concession and are required to terminate early, don't trust the lessor to calculate the buy-out amount. Check it by calling your local bank and asking them to do a calculation for you. Give them the amount of the loan, the interest rate, the term (your lease's term) and the number of months remaining. They'll give you a pay-off amount. This is your magic number.

Negotiating a favorable lease term.

When a pre-packaged lease is offered on a car, the lease term is usually set by the dealer or manufacturer. If this term is not attractive to you (too long, too short), by all means, ask for a different money factor and more or less depreciation due to a change in residual value.

Commentary on Step 6

6. Review and execute the lease agreement.

A vehicle lease agreement will be completed by the lessor after all terms and conditions are agreed upon. Vehicle lease agreements are very much like apartment or office space leases in that they are quite standardized from one to the next. Thus, any changes to the basic agreement must be included on the agreement, or on some type of rider to the agreement. Most lease agreements have blank spaces where variables are entered (i.e., residual value, advance payment amount, security deposit amount, lease length, mileage allowance, etc.).

Once the document has been completed, do not hesitate to have an attorney review it, particularly if changes to the basic language have been made. Should there come a time when a dispute arises over a changed clause, language must be clear as to its intent and meaning.

Before you are asked to sign the lease agreement, the lessor will usually want 24 hours to do a credit check on you. If the vehicle is being leased by your company, the company's credit will also be checked. It is not unusual for the lessor to request a personal financial statement, just as a bank would. However, some lessors will request a copy of the first page of your most recent federal income tax return. The lessor may also request a copy of your company's most current balance sheet and income statement. You are not obligated to produce these documents. If other reliable forms of credit information are available, tell the lessor to use them. Offer as little personal information as possible without jeopardizing or delaying the transaction.

Summary on negotiating

This book cannot tell you which of the above points to negotiate, nor can it predict how successful you'll be. The most important thing to remember is this: It's your money on the table. Don't be the least bit hesitant to play hardball. If you don't like the terms being quoted, walk away. The lessor who wants the deal badly enough will come back to you with a counter proposal.

Remember: "He who wants it bad enough...loses."

5

HOW TO DETERMINE IF A LEASE IS RIGHT FOR YOU

Comparing A Lease Quotation To Conventional Bank Financing

Now that you have learned the basics needed to negotiate a favorable lease, the question becomes: Should I lease or purchase? Unfortunately, the answer is more complex than the question suggests. This chapter deals with the various issues which may impact upon your decision-making process. However, do not expect the book to make your decision, for there is no way to quantify all the issues. Consider that several issues are purely emotional while others are almost entirely economic.

Dealing with the economic issues is relatively straight-forward. A simple calculation can help you compare the costs of leasing to those of conventional bank financing. With this calculation, you should have no trouble in determining whether leasing is a viable economic alternative. To make this calculation, simply fill in the blank areas in Table 4 after you have been out to the dealers of your choice, have negotiated a rock-bottom purchase price and lease terms, and have checked out the various sources of conventional financing.

TABLE 4

Considerations	Lease	Financed Purchase
Costs incurred at the beginning of the transaction:		
Security deposit:	$ _____	$ Not applicable
Down payment:	Not applicable	_____
Sales tax:	_____	_____
Additional insurance: [1]	_____	_____
PLUS		
Costs incurred during the term of the transaction:		
Loan principal:	Not applicable	_____
Loan interest:	Not applicable	_____
Lease payments:	_____	Not applicable
PLUS		
Other costs:		
Lost earnings on downpayment: [2]	Not applicable	_____
Lost earnings on lease deposits: [3]	_____	Not applicable
Extraordinary fees and charges: [4]	_____	Not applicable
SUBTOTAL:	$ _____	$ _____

(TABLE 4 CONTINUED NEXT PAGE)

MINUS

Recaptured costs:
Security deposit refund: _____   Not applicable
Residual value: Not applicable   _____

EQUALS

TOTAL COST: $ _____ $ _____

Footnotes to Comparison of Costs Table

[1] You may be required by the lessor to carry more insurance than is required in your state. There is an associated extra cost.

[2] Loss of interest on downpayment. Enter the simple interest you would earn if deposited in a bank for an equivalent number of years.

[3] Loss of interest on security deposit. Assumes no interest will be paid by the lessor. If you do receive interest, include it with the security deposit refund under "Recaptured Costs."

[4] Add in cost such as excess mileage, disposition fee, but not costs such as licence and registration which are the same for both the lease and financed purchase.

Sample Problem: Compare The Economics of Leasing Versus Bank Financing

The problem in Table 5 will help you visualize the concept of making a direct financial comparison between leasing and financing via a bank loan. For this illustration, we will use a purchase price of $26,000.00, 5% sales tax, a 20% down payment and 10.5% APR on the auto loan, and a 48 month lease. We will also use 6% as the current rate of interest on money market accounts and a 28% tax bracket.

TABLE 5

Considerations	Lease	Financed Purchase
Costs incurred at the beginning of the transaction:		
Security deposit:	$ 500.00	Not applicable
Down payment:	Not applicable	$ 5,200.00
Sales tax:	In lease payment	1,300.00
Additional insurance:	None	None
PLUS		
Costs incurred during the term of the transaction:		
Loan principal:	Not applicable	20,800.00
Loan interest:	Not applicable	4,432.00
Lease payments:	24,000.00	Not applicable
PLUS		
Other costs:		
Lost earnings on downpayment:	Not applicable	1,364.88
Lost earnings on lease deposits:	131.23	Not applicable
Extraordinary fees and charges:	None	Not applicable
SUBTOTAL:	**$ 24,631.23**	**$ 33,096.88**

(TABLE 5 CONTINUED NEXT PAGE)

MINUS

Recaptured costs:

Security deposit refund:	500.00	Not applicable
Residual value:	Not applicable	10,000.00

EQUALS

TOTAL COST:	**$ 24,131.23**	**$ 23,096.88**

In the above example, leasing is more costly by about $1,034.35. Over a four year period, you are looking at a $258.58 per year, or $21.54 per month differential. However, your monthly cash outlay will be about $25.00 less with the lease. Plus, you won't have any costs associated with selling or trading-in your used car four years down the road. So, you may be wise to lease in order to lower your monthly payments.

You might also wish to lease because there's no down payment required as with a bank loan. In the example, a 20% down payment requirement means you must hand-over $5,200.00 in cash to the dealer, with the balance coming from loan proceeds. Even with only 10% down, your cash outlay is $2,600.00 versus zero with a lease. For some people, eliminating the down payment means being able to drive away in a nicer car and still afford the monthly payments. As in any form of financial commitment, one should avoid overextending one's self at all cost. Being car-poor is a fate far worse than being house-poor. Houses generally appreciate, cars generally don't.

Once you have made your economic comparison, you'll want to sit back and contemplate a few of the emotional issues. For example, how many years do you really want to drive the same car? A leased car is usually far more difficult and costly to trade in mid-lease. A bank-financed car would probably be a better choice.

Or, how big is your ego? Must you absolutely, positively have that top-of-the-line, fully-loaded, luxury model? If so, a lease may get you the car you want where you may have to settle for a more modest model via the bank loan route.

Ask yourself how tough you'll be on your car. If your answer is very tough, you'd best stay away from leasing. The chances are good that a lessor will nail you with a ton of extra charges at turn-in time. Items such as excess tire wear, body damage, excess mileage, mechanical problems, a dirty interior, rust and corrosion, and failure to comply with the manufacturer's suggested service program can - and probably will - cost you out-of-pocket. True, most of these problems will also occur on your purchased car, but they may not affect the car's ultimate trade-in value quite so dramatically as they could on a leased car whose lessor wants to get picky-picky-picky.

In summary, leasing isn't for everyone. Yet, experts predict that nearly half the cars sold by 1995 will be under lease. That's because leasing does hold many advantages for a large segment of our population. You may or may not include yourself. The tough part is deciding.

COMPARING LEASE QUOTATIONS - APPLES TO APPLES

In order to assure that you are receiving the best possible terms and conditions on your lease, it is important to compare offers on exactly the same basis. To make the task easier, use the following worksheets to record pertinent data. Each worksheet will also serve as a checklist to be sure you have asked each lessor for all necessary information.

Basic Information Common To All Dealers/Lessors:

1. Vehicle Make: _____

2. Vehicle Model: _____

3. Options Package:_____

4. Manufacturer's Suggested
   Retail Price (MSRP): $ _____

Potamkin Leasing

Specializing In Leasing & Creative Financing Of All Makes & Models

787 Eleventh Avenue at 55th St.
New York, NY 10019
(212) 603-7070
Private Line: (212) 603-7035
FAX (212) 603-7245

MR. CHETT
LEASING MANAGER

WORKSHEET Dealer/Lessor #1

Name: _____

Sales Person: _____ Phone: _____

1. List Basics of Lease Payment

A) Vehicle sticker price: $ _____

B) Vehicle purchase price: _____

C) Trade-In (cap reduction):   _____

D) Vehicle residual value: _____

E) Depreciation amount [A−D]:   _____

F) Lease rate or lease fee amount: _____

G) Monthly payment: _____

2. Calculate Planned Lease Cost

A) Monthly Payment x Months on Lease: _____

B) Taxes: _____

C) Lease initiation fee: _____

D) Title & registration fee: _____

E) Disposition fee: _____

F) Excess mileage charge: *   _____

G) Interest lost on security deposit: _____

TOTAL PLANNED LEASE COST: $ _____

* Estimate mileage over allowance and multiply by per-mile charge.

WORKSHEET Dealer/Lessor #2

Name: _____

Sales Person: _____ Phone: _____

1. List Basics of Lease Payment

A) Vehicle sticker price: $ _____

B) Vehicle purchase price: _____

C) Trade-In (cap reduction):   _____

D) Vehicle residual value: _____

E) Depreciation amount [A − D]:   _____

F) Lease rate or lease fee amount: _____

G) Monthly payment: _____

2. Calculate Planned Lease Cost

A) Monthly Payment x Months on Lease: _____

B) Taxes: _____

C) Lease initiation fee: _____

D) Title & registration fee: _____

E) Disposition fee: _____

F) Excess mileage charge: *   _____

G) Interest lost on security deposit: _____

TOTAL PLANNED LEASE COST: $ _____

* Estimate mileage over allowance and multiply by per-mile charge.

WORKSHEET Dealer/Lessor #3

Name: _____

Sales Person: _____ Phone: _____

1. List Basics of Lease Payment

A) Vehicle sticker price: $ _____

B) Vehicle purchase price: _____

C) Trade-In (cap reduction):   _____

D) Vehicle residual value: _____

E) Depreciation amount [A−D]:   _____

F) Lease rate or lease fee amount: _____

G) Monthly payment: _____

2. Calculate Planned Lease Cost

A) Monthly Payment x Months on Lease: _____

B) Taxes: _____

C) Lease initiation fee: _____

D) Title & registration fee: _____

E) Disposition fee: _____

F) Excess mileage charge: *   _____

G) Interest lost on security deposit: _____

TOTAL PLANNED LEASE COST: $ _____

* Estimate mileage over allowance and multiply by per-mile charge.

HOW TO FIND THE HIDDEN INTEREST CHARGES IN A LEASE

Most leases are quoted with a monthly payment amount. However, lessors are not obligated to tell you what interest rate is being charged on the depreciation cost. You can easily figure this out, enabling you to equate the rate to current bank interest rates. Here is how:

Situation: Whitewall Motors offers you the following terms on the purchase of a flashy, new four door sedan:

Suggested retail price	$ 25,500.00
Purchase price:	22,450.00
Trade-In offer:	6,500.00
Sales tax:	957.00
Title and license:	75.00

You have done your comparative shopping and feel that Whitewall's prices are acceptable. You advise the sales person of your desire to lease the new car for 48 months. A 48 month lease price is provided to you:

Monthly payment:	$ 308.41
Residual value:	6,959.00

To determine the lease rate or lease fee and its hidden interest charge:

1) Determine the monthly depreciation cost.

Purchase price:	$ 22,450.00	
Less: Trade-in:	-6,500.00	
Sub total:		$ 15,950.00
Plus: Taxes & title:	1,032.00	
Sub total:		16,982.00
Less: Residual value:	-6,959.00	
Depreciation cost:		10,023.00
Divide depreciation by 48:		208.81

2) Subtract monthly depreciation from the monthly payment to determine the monthly lease rate or lease fee.

Monthly lease payment:	308.41	
Less: Depreciation cost:	-208.81	
Lease rate or fee:		99.60

3) Determine what annual percentage rate would equal $99.60 when applied to the "total money" of the lease.
   In this example, total money equals purchase price ($16,982) plus residual ($6,959)..
   Formula: $23,941.00 × ? = 99.60
            ? = 99.60 ÷ $ 23,941.00
            ? = .00416

4) Multiply .00416 by 24 to get annual percentage rate of 0.099 or 9.9%. You know that bank interest rates on car loans are currently about 10%, so you feel comfortable that your lease rate is fair.

BE SURE

Here are a few additional nuggets of information which you should BE SURE to keep in mind before deciding to lease and in negotiating for the best lease possible.

1. Be sure the car you lease car is fully warranted

Beware! Some car manufacturers will not transfer warranty rights on a leased car when an independent leasing company or bank is the lessor. You need to be absolutely certain that all warranties are assignable to you and that the manufacturer and lessor both guarantee your warranty rights. Get it in writing. Don't be hesitant to ask an attorney to check into this for you. The 1976 Consumer Leasing Act requires the lessor to disclose whether standard warranties are available from the manufacturer or whether additional warranties are provided by the lessor.

2. Be sure your insurance covers a total loss or theft

Most leases state that the lessee assumes all risk for vehicle loss or damage. Usually, the lessee is required to give the lessor notice of the casualty within 30 days. This normally leads to an involuntary early termination of the lease and the lessee becomes obligated to pay-off the lease per the terms of the agreement. As you know from our discussion about early termination, this can be very costly.

A leased car that's destroyed in an accident or stolen and never recovered will cost more to replace than insurance normally provides. Your insurance company may offer a special policy to cover the difference. It's often referred to as "gap" insurance. The annual premiums are based on a percentage of the monthly lease payment. Check it out.

3. Be sure you and your lessor agree on the definition of "wear and tear resulting from normal use."

All closed-end lease contracts state that the lessee is required

To return the vehicle without excess wear and tear. But nobody seems to have defined what is excessive. Generally, parking lot door or fender nicks and dings are normal. But, how many are "too many?" A broken windshield clearly isn't normal wear and you'll have to pay for its repair. But, how about a rusted exhaust system? Tire wear to less than 1/8 inch of tread is also considered excessive so you'll foot the bill for new rubber. But, how about worn upholstery? Who pays for a lens on a turn signal if a rock breaks the plastic?

To the extent that your lease contract contains specific language which defines excessive wear and tear, and assigns responsibility for repair, you'll be better off. And watch out for contract language that can cost you. There's a big difference between a car in "good or clean retail condition" and one in "average retail condition." Average is what you should insist upon.

4. Be sure you lease as close to the beginning of a model year as possible.

Most new cars are introduced in the fall of the year prior to the model year. If possible, complete your deal during the fall or early winter. It's customary for manufacturers to raise prices after January 1st. Also, the residual value used to figure your lease can drop as much as 5% in a twelve month period. You may also want to do your deal as close to the end of a month as possible. Dealers have sales quotas and it's almost a sure bet that they'll be scrambling for deals as the end of the month approaches.

5. Be sure you avoid year-end "fire sale" special lease deals.

Most manufacturers will promote special deals just before a new model year to clear current model year inventory. While the deal may sound attractive, remember that the sticker price is at its highest at year-end, residual is at its lowest, and the car loses significant value the day the new models are introduced.

6. Be sure you negotiate your buy-out price.

If you decide to buy your car at lease termination, don't think that the buy-out price in your contact is etched in stone. It's negotiable even though the dealer or leasing company will tell you the price is "in the contract." Remember, they have certain costs to absorb in taking the car back from you, refurbishing it, and trying to resell it. A reasonable offer on your part may be worth their while as well as yours.

A FINAL THOUGHT

You now have all the information needed to understand the leasing process, and, with a bit of gumption, to negotiate a less-costly, more favorable lease. You also have the means to determine whether or not leasing is right for you.

A very dear friend and long-time business associate once told me, "Rick, you can't crap a crapper." What he was saying is simply to avoid trying to beat the experts at their own game. The people who sell cars for a living know the ropes and, given the opportunity, can tie most consumers into tiny, little knots. They can be especially unmerciful on "wiseguys."

The best piece of advice this author can give is: use your knowledge defensively. After all, the best offense is a great defense. Let the dealer or lessor take the initiative and make the offers. Then, use the information presented in this book to **analyze** the quality of the offers. Be prepared to walk away from a deal if it isn't comfortable. Be prepared to know when a deal is right.

Above all, be patient. Remember, the seller's goal is to **sell** the car. Your goal is to make certain he sells it to you for less money and on better terms.

INDEX

ABOUT THE AUTHOR

Richard L. Kaye is president of a Chicago-area business-to-business marketing communications agency. Over the years, his firm has had several clients in the leasing industry, including one that specialized in automobile fleet leasing. He has also worked with retail automobile dealers, and financial institutions.

Kaye has had numerous articles published on advertising and marketing, and serves on governing committees of several trade associations including the American Association of Advertising Agencies. He is also an active trustee of the Chicago-Northern Illinois chapter of the National Multiple Sclerosis Society.

And, yes, Kaye has leased several cars over the years. The lease that pleased him most was on a 1986 Audi 5000 which he leased for three years from late 1985 to 1988. While he had the car, Audi values plummeted due to unintended acceleration problems. At the lease's end, he turned the car in and walked away, unscathed. Had he owned the car, Kaye claims that he would have lost a bundle.

Lease Your Car For Less is Kaye's first commercial publishing venture.